D1283123

MONSTERS

Dragons

by Catherine M. Petrini

KIDHAVEN PRESS

An imprint of Thomson Gale, a part of The Thomson Corporation

THOMSON

GALE

Detroit • New York • San Francisco • New Haven, Conn. • Waterville, Maine • London

© 2007 Thomson Gale, a part of The Thomson Corporation.

Thomson and Star Logo are trademarks and Gale and KidHaven Press are registered trademarks used herein under license.

For more information, contact
KidHaven Press
27500 Drake Rd.
Farmington Hills, MI 48331-3535
Or you can visit our Internet site at http://www.gale.com

Picture Credits:
Cover: © Kelly-Mooney Photography/CORBIS; akg-images, 5, 20 ;© Reinhard Dirsher/Alamy, 11 ;© Mary Evans Picture Library/Alamy, 17, 19, 26, 29 ;Giraudon/Art Resource, N.Y., 25 ;Réunion des Musées Nationaux/Art Resource, N.Y., 30 ;Bridgeman Art Library, 18 ;© Robert Holmes/CORBIS, 12 ;© Keren Su/CORBIS, 23 ;Paramount/Disney/The Kobal Collection, 14 ;Mary Evans Picture Library, 6 ;Photofestnyc, 33, 34, 37

LIBRARY OF CONGRESS CATALOGING-IN-PUBLICATION DATA
Petrini, Catherine M.
Dragons / by Catherine M. Petrini.
p. cm. — (Monsters)
Includes bibliographical references and index.
ISBN 13: 978-0-7377-3163-7 (lib. : alk. paper)
ISBN 10: 0-7377-3163-X (lib. : alk. paper)
1. Dragons—Juvenile literature. I. Title.
GR830.D7P48 2006
398.24'54—dc22
2006023032

Printed in the United States

CONTENTS

CHAPTER 1

Beyond Here Be Dragons

Early mapmakers marked the edges of the known world with a warning: "Beyond here be dragons." Nobody knew what lurked in unexplored places. But in a time when most people stayed close to home, they assumed that unfamiliar lands held dangerous things. One of the most powerful and alien beasts they could imagine was a dragon. In stories throughout the world, dragons were huge, lizard-like **predators**. Because many dragons could fly, they could pounce without warning and kill people. They breathed smoke, fire, or poisonous fumes. Some ate humans. Today, we know that dragons are fictional—imaginary creatures. But hundreds of years ago, most people believed in dragons—both as real, living animals and as symbols of the wild, uncontrollable, and deadly forces of nature.

No matter where they were created, dragon stories from around the world are remarkably similar. People of many times and places spun tales about dragons. Most dragons share some common traits.

Defining a Dragon

In most dragon myths, dragons are giant lizards with long tails. Their bodies are covered with tough, shiny scales. Their necks are long and flexible, and some

Dragons are often pictured as winged, fire-breathing creatures with sharp teeth and claws, and a long tail.

dragons have two or more heads. Dragons may have two or four legs, and many also have leathery, batlike wings that allow them to fly. Dragons slash at their prey with big, sharp claws. They rip into meat–or enemies–with huge, pointy teeth. Some dragons have horns on their heads or crests running along the top of their heads and down their spines. Many Asian dragons have beards.

New World explorers told of seeing dragons in their travels through North America.

Combination Creatures

Some cultures describe dragons as having body parts that look like several different kinds of animals—or even humans. Jorge Luis Borges, author of *The Book of Imaginary Beings*, speaks of the dragon's "nine resemblances: its horns are not unlike those of a stag, its head that of a camel, its eyes those of a devil, its neck that of a snake, its belly that of a clam, its scales those of a fish, its talons those of an eagle, its footprints those of a tiger, and its ears those of an ox."[1]

Most dragons that look like a combination of creatures are not quite so mixed up. For example, a legend of the Seminole people of Florida tells of a water dragon that was part cat and part reptile. More complicated was the body of the Piasa dragon, which the Algonquin of the Mississippi Valley painted on rocks near treacherous parts of the river. A seventeenth-century French explorer discovered drawings of this dragon. He claimed it had the horns of a deer, the face of a man, blood-red eyes, the beard of a tiger, leathery wings, a scale-covered body with a long tail, and smoke pouring from its nostrils!

"Dragons of Sundry Colors"

Most dragons are brightly colored, sometimes with spots or other markings. "There are dragons of sundry colors, for some are black, some red, some

The colors of Chinese dragons have special meanings. Yellow dragons were thought to rule the summer season.

of an ash-color, some yellow,"[2] declared Edward Topsell, a seventeenth-century **zoologist**. Across cultures, green, red, and black dragons are the most common, though they also come in white, blue, and yellow. Dragons of the Americas tend to be greenish, while Tibetan dragons are always red. In polar regions, dragons are white, sometimes with a bluish tinge, to help them blend into the icy landscape.

In some cultures, dragon colors have special meaning. In ancient China, the Green Dragon, or spirit dragon, lived in the east and controlled the spring. The south had two dragons, the Red Dragon and the Yellow Dragon, who together ruled the summer. The White Dragon of the west was in charge of autumn. And the Black Dragon, who lived in the north, controlled the winter months.

Anne McCaffrey, a well-known author of modern dragon novels, writes about colorful dragons in a world called Pern. In her Dragonriders of Pern books, the dragons follow a unique color scheme. Golden dragons, always female, are queen dragons. They are the rarest, largest, and most magnificent. Bronze dragons are the biggest and strongest of all the other dragons; only a bronze dragon can mate with a queen. Pernese dragons may also be brown, blue, or green. Greens, the most common, are also the smallest, starting at about 65 feet long (20m). But the largest Pernese dragons can be up to 150 feet long (45m), the size of a jet plane.

Dinosaur Bones and Primal Fears

McCaffrey thinks dragons probably did exist in some form. "I think there may have been dragons somewhere, but they died out along with the dinosaurs. Mankind simply has never seen any skeletons,"[3] she says. If real dragons did live in the past and were found all over the world, that would explain why cultures all over the world describe dragons that look so much alike.

Some real-life lizards that look like dragons still live in Indonesia. These animals, called Komodo dragons, are named for their home on Komodo Island and for the legendary dragons they resemble. Komodo dragons do not fly. But like imaginary dragons, they are fierce reptiles with scaly bodies, long tails, sharp claws, razor-sharp teeth, and strong legs. They live in underground caves. And like fictional dragons that breathe out deadly fumes, the Komodo dragon's saliva is poisonous to other animals.

Another explanation for the similarity of dragon stories around the world is that dragon myths were fueled by discoveries of dinosaur bones. Early people found the bones and created stories to explain the unfamiliar beasts.

Other **dragonologists** believe dragons share recognizable traits because the idea of dragons grew out of deep-seated fears shared by people around the world. In his book, *An Instinct for Dragons*, David Jones argues that the dragon is a mix of predators

that terrified early humans. He came up with this theory while studying monkeys. He was examining pictures of three predators that attack some monkeys. "Suddenly, in my mind's eye," he says, "the three predator images merged. The leopard body took on the outer look of the python, resulting in a large reptilian body with four clawed feet and a mouth full of sharp teeth. When the wings of the martial eagle attached to the shoulders of the blended leopard/python, I saw a dragon!"[4] He believes that early humans also feared large predatory cats, deadly snakes, and birds of prey. From those

The fierce-looking Komodo dragon (pictured) is a giant lizard found on Komodo Island in Indonesia.

Some dragon stories may have come from the discovery of dinosaur skeletons such as this one.

fears, they created stories about dragons. The late scientist Carl Sagan had a similar theory. He suggested that dragons sprang from mammals' genetic memory of dinosaurs. Those memories were etched into the minds of our earliest mammal ancestors, small animals whose terror and awe of the huge, deadly reptiles still haunt the human mind.

However dragon stories began, it is clear that those stories grew and spread. Eventually, people all over the world believed in dragons, and most were sure they knew exactly what these awesome creatures were like.

CHAPTER 2

THE BEHAVIOR OF DRAGONS

Dragon stories from around the world depict similar dragon behaviors. For instance, most dragons fly. They are often pictured soaring high in the air, where they hunt like birds of prey and swoop down to snatch deer, goats, or people. Some dragons even mate in midair. Chinese and Japanese dragons are godlike creatures that can launch themselves from their watery homes and fly up into the sky—even though they have no wings.

Some dragon species that live underwater cannot fly. Stories of flightless dragons come from various parts of the world, including India, Scandinavia, and North America. Water dragons are expert swimmers and

In this scene from a movie, a dragon shoots flames from its mouth before it swoops down to catch its prey.

divers that eat smaller sea creatures and are often blamed for floods. They may be the same beasts that appear in sea serpent myths. In fact, some dragonologists believe a dragon is behind the legend of the Loch Ness Monster—a mysterious, long-necked creature who has been sighted in a lake in Scotland.

"SOME VAPOROUS AND VENOMOUS BREATH"

Drawings of flying dragons show them breathing out flames that blacken the ground beneath them.

Deadly breath is a typical trait of dragons. Many shoot out fire that can scorch an entire town. Others belch smoke or poisonous fumes that can kill a person instantly. Such myths are especially popular in places where fire, smoke, or steam rises naturally from the earth, such as near volcanoes, geysers, and swamps. Some ancient people explained these mysteries with stories of dragons that lived in underground caves and snorted out flames or vapor.

In early dragon stories, a dragon's fiery or poisonous breath was accepted as fact. Topsell included dragons in his seventeenth-century books about real wildlife. He cited the dragons of Phrygia, now part of Turkey. When a Phrygian dragon is hungry, "they turn themselves toward the west, and, gaping wide, with the force of their breath they draw into their mouth the birds that fly overhead. It is probable that some vaporous and venomous breath is sent up from the dragon; and the birds, astonished, fall down into the dragon's mouth." [5]

Even earlier, the eighth-century **epic** *Beowulf* described a fire-breathing dragon that has inspired European folklore for more than 1,200 years. The epic tells how Beowulf, a Danish hero,

> *Felt the heat*
> *Of the dragon's breath, flooding down*
> *Through the hidden entrance, too hot for anyone*
> *To stand, a streaming current of fire*
> *And smoke that blocked all passage.* [6]

Fire from the Sky

As time went on and people learned scientific explanations for the natural world, they tried to explain dragon fire. Modern dragonologists still try to explain it. Some of these studies are just for fun, but others are serious efforts to determine if dragons might have ever existed. Biologist Peter Hogarth theorizes that real-life dragons might have had sacs filled with **hydrogen** inside their bodies. These sacs would act like balloons to keep the dragons aloft, and—because hydrogen burns easily—would fuel their fiery breath, which they would ignite by eating a flammable mineral, platinum.

McCaffrey has a similar explanation. In her novels, Pernese dragons have a second stomach. This stomach processes firestone, a kind of rock on the world of Pern. Dragons chew and swallow firestone, which contains a flammable gas. When they puff the gas out, it hits oxygen in the air and ignites into flame. Interestingly, McCaffrey's dragons do not use this fire to burn humans. They use it to help the people of Pern fight a deadly life-form known as Thread. Other theories about dragon fire suggest that a dragon breathes fire because of methane or other flammable gases made in its body. It might set fire to the gas by forcing a huge puff of air past a tiny spark—like the pilot light on a stove or furnace—that always burns in the back of its throat.

Dragons

An engraving depicts Beowulf using a shield and sword to fight off a dragon's deadly breath of flames.

Long, Sharp, and Lethal

Dragons also kill with their long, sharp claws and teeth. Most dragons are carnivorous. Depending on their location, they might eat livestock, wild animals, or even humans. Chinese dragons are especially fond of roasted swallows. Some central Asian dragons prefer two-humped camels. And a few dragon breeds are vegetarian; the faerie dragon is a small, metallic-colored vegetarian dragon that appears in stories from tropical and subtropical regions around the world. But even vegetarian dragons have dangerous claws and teeth. According to Topsell, they might use them to slice into fruits and vegetables.

Castles, Caves, and Treasure Troves

Most dragons are solitary animals, living as far from people as their dietary needs allow. They might inhabit underground caverns, mountaintop lairs, swamps, or the bottoms of rivers or lakes. A kind of European forest dragon called a knucker makes its home in deep holes in the ground, called knuckerholes. Other dragons live more lavishly, even in castles.

Dragons are also depicted living near treasures and watching over them. Dragons' treasures can take

Even in sleep, this dragon guards the treasure of precious jewels in its cave.

In the greek myth of Jason and the Argonauts, Jason attempts to steal the dragon's treasure—the Golden Fleece.

various forms. The cavern homes of many European dragons–including Beowulf's famous dragon–overflow with gold and precious jewels. The underwater palaces of some Asian dragons are filled with treasures and protected by magic.

Dragon Magic

Instead of guarding a trove of treasure, other dragons guard a single priceless artifact. Often, it is a jewel that holds magical power and is the source of the dragon's **supernatural** abilities. Sometimes the magical jewel is worn by the dragon or is part of the dragon's body, often embedded in its forehead. In Asian cultures, the jewel may be a magical pearl held under the dragon's mouth. In Ethiopia, a powerful stone called the Dracontias lodges inside the dragon's brain. It retains its

The Norse hero Sigurd kills the evil dragon Fafnir. Sigurd gained special powers after eating the dragon's heart.

powers only if removed while the dragon is alive. In many cultures, the dragon slayer who steals a dragon's jewel inherits its magical powers.

Other dragon parts are also thought to have special powers, especially their bones and blood. In fact, in many stories, dragons are hunted by humans who prize their body parts as medicine and as a source of magic. Ancient Greek myths claim that a dragon's teeth, planted in the ground like seeds, will grow into an army of fierce warriors. And **Norse** mythology tells of an evil man named Fafnir who transformed himself into a dragon so he could guard a trove of stolen treasure. As a dragon, he lived happily with his gold until the hero Sigurd slew him. Then Sigurd cut out Fafnir's heart and roasted it. When blood seeped out, Sigurd accidentally spilled some on his finger and touched his mouth. Suddenly he could understand the language of birds.

But in most stories, the magic in a dragon's blood or tooth cannot make a person as powerful as a live dragon. Dragon magic covers many kinds of supernatural talent and uncanny wisdom. Some dragons have the ability to read human minds, while others can change their own appearance or become invisible. In some cultures, dragons can paralyze victims who stare into their glowing eyes. Other dragons have magical healing powers they use to help humans who are sick or injured.

Their extraordinary bodies and mysterious talents make all dragons powerful and awesome creatures.

CHAPTER 3

DRAGON GODS AND DEVILS

In mythologies around the world, a dragon can be good or evil. In Asia, for example, dragons are honored as gods. In other cultures—most famously, in medieval Europe—they are reviled as the embodiment of evil.

THE DRAGON KINGS OF CHINA

One of the earliest known dragon stories in any culture is set on the banks of China's Yellow River. That is where a dragon met a man named Fu Hsi in 2962 B.C. and tutored him in the secrets of civilization. The dragon taught him about writing, fishing, making music, raising animals, and using a compass. Fu Hsi, now considered the first dragonologist, brought the lessons back to his people. This dragon was friendly. It was the creator of Chinese civilization and one of the world's first dragon gods.

Ever since the dragon's gift of knowledge to Fu Hsi, the Chinese have honored dragons as gods. Around 220 B.C., the five-clawed dragon became the symbol of Chinese imperial power. The emperor claimed himself to be the "True Dragon"– descended from dragons and therefore also a god.

The five-clawed dragon of China was the emperor's personal symbol.

At one time, only the emperor and his family were allowed to wear robes that showed five-clawed dragons. People who were not royal could wear only dragons with four claws or fewer. But even the lower classes relied on dragons for luck and prosperity.

Chinese dragons are usually kind to those who show respect. They control the weather and bring needed rain. But they can also be moody, stirring up storms and floods. Despite their awe-inspiring powers, Chinese dragons do have a weakness: Like other Asian dragons, they are afraid of centipedes!

Even today, dragons hold a special place in Chinese culture. Dragon images are paraded in Chinese New Year festivities to scare away evil spirits and bring good luck in the coming year. Every twelfth year of the Chinese calendar is the Year of the Dragon, and children born during these years are said to be blessed with health, wealth, and a long life.

THE GREEN-FEATHERED SERPENT GOD

Before the arrival of Europeans, native cultures of Mexico and Central America worshipped a god known to the Aztecs as Quetzalcoatl, or "green-feathered serpent." This dragon had feathers as well as scales.

Quetzalcoatl played many roles in the lives of the Aztecs. Revered for his wisdom, Quetzalcoatl invented books and the calendar and was the first

Quetzalcoatl, the green-feathered serpent god of the Aztecs, is pictured here devouring a man.

to give corn to the people. He was also the Aztec god of fertility and rain. Unlike some of the harsher gods of the region, he loved peace and hated human sacrifices. He was so important to the Aztecs and other local cultures that some of their rulers took the name Quetzalcoatl and claimed to be the god in human form.

"A Blazing Crest upon Its Forehead"

Not all dragon gods were forces for good. One of the most ancient dragon gods, Tiamat, embodied

chaos and the tempestuous power of nature, especially of storms and the sea. Tablets dating back nearly 4,000 years describe her as a key player in the creation story of ancient Babylon (now Iraq). According to the myth, Tiamat existed in the beginning, when the world was nothing but turbulent water. She was slain in an epic battle by her son Marduk. Then Marduk created the Earth and everything on it.

Less powerful but still capable of controlling floods and storms is the Uktena dragon of the southeastern United States. The Uktena lurks in rivers and in high, lonely passes of the Great Smoky Mountains,

Ancient Babylonian tablets show Marduk bringing peace to the world by slaying Tiamat, the dragon goddess of chaos.

where it is greatly feared by the Cherokee people. The Uktena wreaks havoc by causing rivers to overflow their banks, drowning people and devastating villages, and also by attacking and killing passersby.

According to author James Mooney, the Uktena is "as large around as a tree trunk, with horns on its head, and a bright, blazing crest like a diamond upon its forehead, and scales glittering like sparks of fire. It has rings or spots of color along its whole length, and can not be wounded except by shooting in the seventh spot from the head, because under this spot are its heart and its life."[7] Few Cherokees survive an encounter with this dragon. But Cherokee legend claims that a warrior who steals the blazing crystal from an Uktena's head will lead a charmed life, with success in hunting, love, and rainmaking—and the ability to see the future.

From Protector to Predator

The most famous European dragons—those of medieval times—were also creatures feared and loathed. But in earlier times, European dragons watched over people instead of preying on them. In some early **pagan** religions, dragons and other serpents were actually symbols of goddesses. Women, especially, were under their protection.

The Red Dragon of Wales, named Ddraig Goch, was the dragon referred to in the legendary King Arthur's inherited title, Pendragon. Arthur's father,

Uther, adopted the name Pendragon and began using the dragon as his family's symbol after seeing a dragon-shaped comet. He believed the comet was a sign of Ddraig Goch's protection for him and his heirs.

Judeo-Christian leaders used the dragon as a symbol of evil to discredit ancient religions, especially those that worshiped goddesses. Christianity and Judaism linked dragons with the forces of evil, even with Satan himself. The book of Revelation, for example, describes a heavenly battle in which a band of good angels triumphs over "a great red dragon, having seven heads and ten horns, and seven crowns upon his heads. . . . And the great dragon was cast out, that old serpent, called the devil, and Satan, which deceiveth the whole world" (12:3-9).

Instead of protecting women, European dragons of the Christian era liked to kidnap and eat them. So knights and saints who rescued maidens from dragons became staples of medieval lore. The most famous of these was Saint George, the patron saint of England.

Saint George and the Dragon of Paganism

Legends about Saint George vary. Some say he was George of Cappadocia, a dragon slayer who, according to thirteenth-century lore, fought and killed a dragon in Libya. But many scholars believe Saint George and George of Cappadocia were two

In this engraving, angels descend from the sky to fight the seven-headed Red Dragon of Revelation.

different people. In any case, a popular medieval legend told of a dragon who terrorized the countryside and was appeased only by offerings of sheep. Then the dragon demanded human children. Each day, a lottery was held to select a child to be eaten. Eventually, the king's daughter was chosen.

Hogarth describes what happened next:

At this moment St. George, in the role of knight errant, makes a timely appearance. He asks the princess what is happening; she tells him, and beseeches him to save himself by fleeing. Naturally, St. George stands his ground and, when the dragon emerges from the lake, smites it with his spear "and hurt him sore." The dragon is so seriously wounded (and possibly so astonished) that it is led meekly back into the city by the princess. St. George makes a brief oration, baptizes the en-

Art from the Middle Ages shows Saint George slaying the dragon that terrorized the countryside.

tire population, and then, with a striking want of Christian forgiveness, lops off the dragon's head.[8]

Another Christian saint who vanquished godlessness in the form of a dragon is Saint Martha of Bethany. She conquered a dragon called the Tarasque, which lived in an underwater cave in France. According to Hogarth, "It was larger than an ox, with a lion's head and teeth, six paws like those of a bear, and a hard skin covered with spikes, ending in a tail of a viper."[9] This dragon was a menace, roiling the river into floods and attacking local residents. One day, while it was eating one of them, Saint Martha sprinkled it with holy water. The dragon instantly reformed its evil ways.

Whether they are good or evil, the one thing all dragons share is power—not only to protect or to destroy, but also the power to capture human imaginations.

Chapter 4

From Puff to Pern: Dragons in Popular Culture

People continue to be intrigued by dragons. They play a part in books and stories, movies, television shows, role-playing games such as Dungeons and Dragons, video games, and music.

People still retell the old stories about dragons. The legends of King Arthur are especially popular. These stories are filled with the adventures of knights such as Sir Lancelot, who slew wicked, fierce dragons to rescue maidens and save terrified villagers. But these classic tales differ from today's dragon stories in a noticeable way: In many modern tales, dragons are harm-less—even friendly.

A Boy and His Dragon

One of the most sympathetic dragons in popular culture is the subject of a hit song. "Puff the Magic Dragon" was written in 1959 and recorded a few years later by the folk group Peter, Paul, and Mary. The song tells of a magical dragon who inspires awe in those who do not know him. Kings and princes bow to him and even pirate ships lower their flags when Puff roars. But Puff is an innocent. He frolics with his best friend Jackie. But eventually, Jackie grows up and moves on to grownup pastimes. And

This animated dragon looks much friendlier than the dragons in stories from centuries ago.

Elliott, the warmhearted dragon of Disney's Pete's Dragon, *plays with his human friend Pete in this movie still.*

the lonely dragon is so broken-hearted that he slips back into his cave.

The idea of dragons as companions to children would have horrified medieval Europeans, but it surfaces often in modern culture. For example, the 1977 Disney film *Pete's Dragon* features a dragon who befriends an orphaned boy. This animated dragon, Elliott, shares some traits with mythological ones. He is large and green, with small wings that help him fly, even while carrying a person on his back. Elliott has some psychic abilities and can make himself invisible. He also can breathe fire, but he does not want to hurt people. He is playful and loyal, though mischievous–like a big, well-intentioned kid. Elliott is described in one song in the movie as having a camel's

head, a crocodile's neck, and a cow's ears–and as being both fish and mammal.

Other dragons who play with children appear in a popular animated television series, shown on PBS stations in the United States. *Dragon Tales* relates the adventures of Emmy and her little brother, Max, typical children who find a magic dragon scale that transports them to Dragon Land. There, they meet four young dragons who become their favorite playmates.

Dragon Tales borrows liberally from dragon lore of various cultures. The dragons are collectors, keeping hoards of childish "treasures"–such as buttons, cupcakes, and frogs–in pouches similar to those in which Australia's **marsupial** dragons carry their young. *Dragon Tales* dragons fly and breathe fire. They include a two-headed dragon that lives in a knuckerhole. And all the young dragons attend classes at the School in the Sky. Their teacher is a wise old Spanish-speaking dragon named Quetzal, a reference to the Aztec dragon god Quetzalcoatl.

DRAGONS OF FEAR AND LOATHING

Not all dragons in modern literature are friendly. In the classic fantasy novel *The Hobbit*, J.R.R. Tolkien writes about Smaug, a fierce and evil dragon who could easily be descended from Beowulf's dragon. It is an enormous, scaly beast, red-gold in color. It flies. It breathes fire. And it revels in riddles. It also has a magical way of controlling people with its smooth voice and hypnotic eyes. Like Beowulf's dragon, Smaug guards a vast treasure of stolen goods in a cavern beneath a mountain and ventures out only to scorch the countryside, lay waste to towns, carry off livestock, and murder humans and the occasional dwarf. Smaug is finally killed by an arrow shot into a soft spot in its chest, where its armorlike scales have been damaged.

Another popular book series draws heavily on northern European dragon lore. Several dragons and dragonlike creatures play prominent roles in J.K. Rowling's Harry Potter books. In fact, one of the villains of the series, a classmate of Harry's at Hogwarts School of Witchcraft and Wizardry, is named Draco, the Greek root of the word "dragon."

In the first book in the series, Harry's friend Hagrid illegally hatches a baby dragon (a Norwegian Ridgeback) from an egg. Hagrid dotes on his new pet, which he names Norbert. But this is not a cute, cuddly baby dragon from Emmy and Max's Dragon Land. This is a deadly, fire-breathing dragon, like the ones of medieval Europe. At Hogwarts, everyone but the beast-loving Hagrid can see that dragons–even newborn dragons–are dangerous. Harry and his friends manage to whisk Norbert off to Romania before the baby dragon

Dragons are an important aspect of the Harry Potter series of books by J.K. Rowling about young wizards.

grows into a serious menace. But in later books, Harry learns firsthand how dangerous dragons can be. The fourth volume, *Harry Potter and the Goblet of Fire,* features a wizardry competition in which each contestant must steal a golden egg from a dragon's lair. Harry faces a foul-tempered Hungarian Horntail, and risks his life in a breakneck midair race to escape the dragon's wrath.

HOOKED ON DRAGONS

Like many dragon enthusiasts, Jane Yolen, author of the Pit Dragon Trilogy, traces her interest in dragons back to childhood. That's when she became hooked on fairy tales, the legends of King

Arthur, and Norse and Germanic myths. Yolen believes dragons have captured people's imaginations through the ages because of their power and wildness: "Dragons are those uncontrollable parts of nature, bigger and meaner and plain unstoppable. One either befriends and understands a dragon, submits to its hugeness, or fights against it, and quite often in any of these three instances – humans die."[10]

For thousands of years, humans have been intrigued and terrified by these fantastic beasts. To this day, dragons live throughout the world in the imaginations of people who believe—or want to believe—in their beauty, in their magic, and in the unbridled power of nature.

NOTES

Chapter 1: Beyond Here Be Dragons

1. Jorge Luis Borges, *The Book of Imaginary Beings.* New York: Avon, 1969, p. 82.
2. Edward Topsell, *Topsell's Histories of Beasts.* Ed., Malcolm Smith. Chicago: Nelson-Hall, 1981, p. 76.
3. Anne McCaffrey, personal interview with the author, July 21, 2005.
4. David E. Jones, *An Instinct for Dragons.* New York: Routledge, 2000, p. 3.

Chapter 2: The Behavior of Dragons

5. Topsell, *Topsell's Histories of Beasts,* p. 78.
6. *Beowulf,* translated by Burton Raffel. New York: New American, 1963, p. 102, lines 2545–49.

Chapter 3: Dragon Gods and Devils

7. James Mooney, *James Mooney's History, Myths, and Sacred Formulas of the Cherokees.* Asheville, NC: Historical Images, 1992, p. 297.
8. Peter Hogarth, *Dragons.* New York: Viking, 1979, pp. 143–44.

9. Hogarth, *Dragons,* p. 150.

Chapter 4: From Puff to Pern: Dragons in Popular Culture

10. Jane Yolen, personal interview with the author, June 5, 2005.

GLOSSARY

chaos: A state of wild confusion.

dragonologists: Experts in the study of dragons.

epic: A long poem that tells a grand story about a historic or legendary hero.

hydrogen: A gas that is lighter than air and catches fire easily.

marsupial: A class of animals whose bodies have pouches for carrying their young.

Norse: Of a northern European region that includes Norway, Sweden, Denmark, Finland, Iceland, and the Faeroe Islands.

pagan: Related to the practice of paganism, the worship of many gods.

predators: Animals that kill and eat other animals.

supernatural: Caused by something that cannot be explained scientifically.

zoologist: A person who studies animals.

FOR FURTHER EXPLORATION

BOOKS

Rhoda Blumberg, *The Truth About Dragons.* New York: Four Winds Press, 1980. This guide to dragons is divided into two parts, one on Western dragons and one on Eastern dragons. Each section describes the dragons' physical appearance, diet, habitat, and social structure. There are also sections on dragons' natural enemies and on cures and charms concerning dragons. Includes a bibliography.

Gail Gibbons, *Behold . . . the Dragons!* New York: Morrow Junior Books, 1999. This colorful picture book provides a brief introduction to dragon lore. It discusses the origins of dragon stories, different types of dragons, famous mythological dragons, and dragons from around the world.

Margaret Hodges, *Saint George and the Dragon: A Golden Legend.* Boston: Little, Brown, 1984. A retelling of the Saint George story. Lavishly illustrated by Trina Schart Hyman, this book won a Caldecott award.

Bobbie Kalman, *Endangered Komodo Dragons*. New York: Crabtree, 2005. They can't fly, but Komodo dragons of Indonesia resemble mythical dragons more closely than any other living lizard. Their habitats, diet, life cycle, survival skills, and interactions with people are all discussed here, with an emphasis on threats to the species' survival. Also included are a glossary, an index, and dozens of color photographs.

Lucille Recht, *Dragons*. New York: Random House, 2004. This overview recounts myths from different countries along with information about what different kinds of dragons look like and where they live. It includes a brief discussion of why people started telling stories about dragons, and is enhanced by Peter Scott's colorful, imaginative pictures.

Dugald Steer, ed., *Dr. Ernest Drake's Dragonology: The Complete Book of Dragons*. Cambridge, MA.: Candlewick, 2003. This popular and charming book pretends to be a copy of an original 1895 volume of dragon research, the culmination of the fictional Dr. Drake's research. Fun and informative, it contains beautifully illustrated sections on dragon life cycles, dragons of the world, spells and charms, tips for tracking dragons, and more. Extras include a sample of "real" dragon skin, a packet of magic dragon dust, and Ernest Drake's library card.

A companion volume is called *The Dragonology Handbook*.

Videos/DVDs

Dragon's World: A Fantasy Made Real, DVD, directed by Justin Hardy. Silver Spring, MD: Animal Planet, 2005. Dragons come alive in this intriguing mock-documentary that follows a team of scientists as they examine dragon remains found preserved in glacial ice on a European mountaintop. This footage is interspersed with lifelike computer-animated "flashbacks" from the dragon's life. Viewers who aren't paying close attention may be fooled into thinking the dragon remains are real! A shorter version of this film appeared on U.S. television, but the DVD version is less choppy and more comprehensive. Don't miss the "making of" film, included on the DVD.

Dragons: Myths and Legends, DVD. New York: A&E Home Video, 2006. This installment of the Ancient Mysteries documentary series explores the evidence for and against the existence of dragons.

Web Sites

Dragon Myths (http://sorrel.humboldt.edu/ ~geog309i/ideas/dragons/dragons.html). This site, based at Humboldt University, offers con-

cise retellings of stories and myths about dragons from Europe, Africa, and Asia.

Here Be Dragons! (www.draconian.com). A resource for everything about dragons: dragon history, dragon art, dragon physiology, dragon's lives, dragon movies, and even dragon tattoos. Interactive features include dragon games and a chat room for dragon lovers.

Sommerland (www.sommerland.org). The most helpful part of this excellent, comprehensive site is a timeline that looks at dragons throughout history. Other sections discuss types of dragons, dragon myths, biblical dragons, and the biology of dragons. The site also features dragon art and a page of links.

INDEX

ABOUT THE AUTHOR

Catherine M. Petrini has written twenty-seven books, most of them fiction or nonfiction for children and teens. A former magazine editor, she is a frequent speaker on writing-related topics and hosts a radio show. She has a bachelor's degree in English from the University of Virginia and a master's in writing from Johns Hopkins University. Her most recent book for KidHaven Press was about Stonehenge.

Indianapolis
Marion County
Public Library

Renew by Phone
269-5222

Renew on the Web
www.imcpl.org

For General Library Information
please call 269-1700